CONTENTS

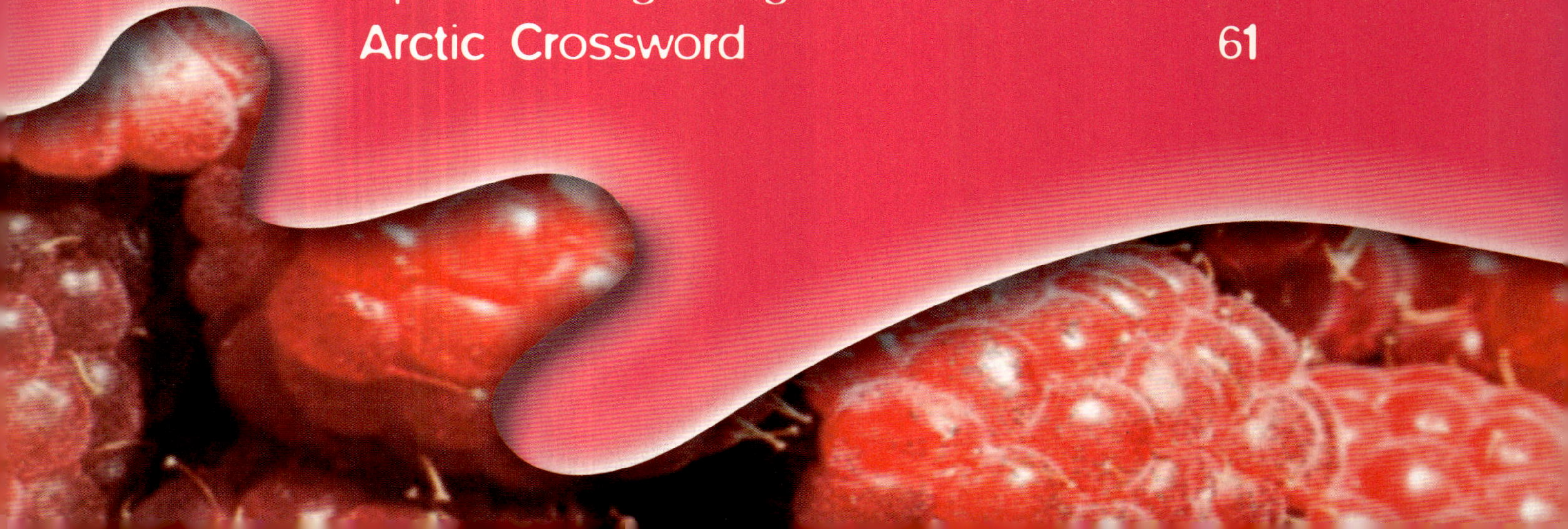

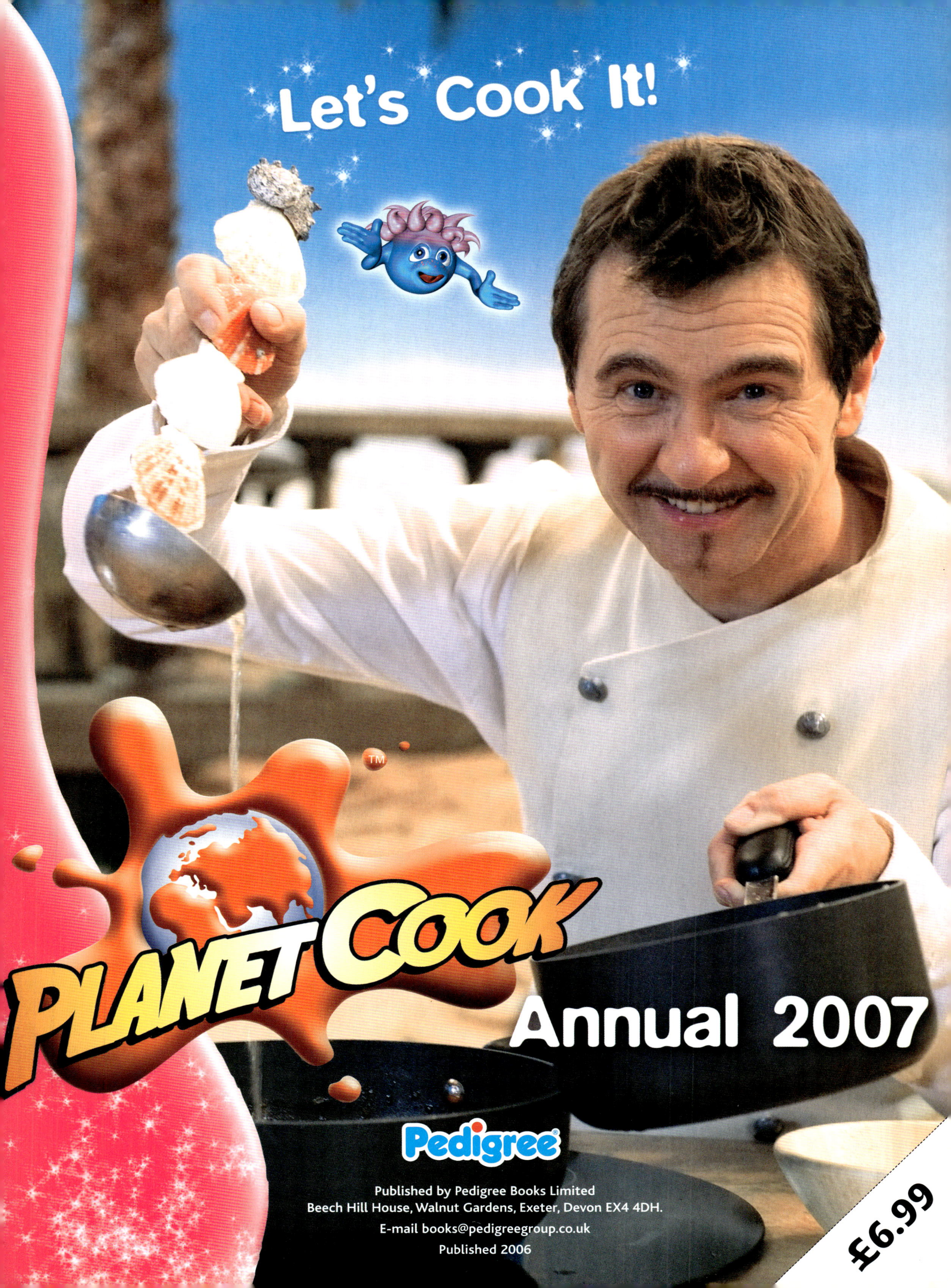

Planet Cook™ Annual 2007

Pedigree

Published by Pedigree Books Limited
Beech Hill House, Walnut Gardens, Exeter, Devon EX4 4DH.
E-mail books@pedigreegroup.co.uk
Published 2006

Captain Cook

He's the hero chef with a mission to make good food fun! A highly experienced chef, Captain Cook creates all the Taste Creations from scratch. He is the master of the kitchen and has the ability to make something completely delicious out of almost nothing.

Bouma

A loveable happy-go-lucky young yeti who likes cooking and helping out where he can but his attention span is quite short. He requires a fair amount of supervision to make sure he doesn't cause any kitchen catastrophes.

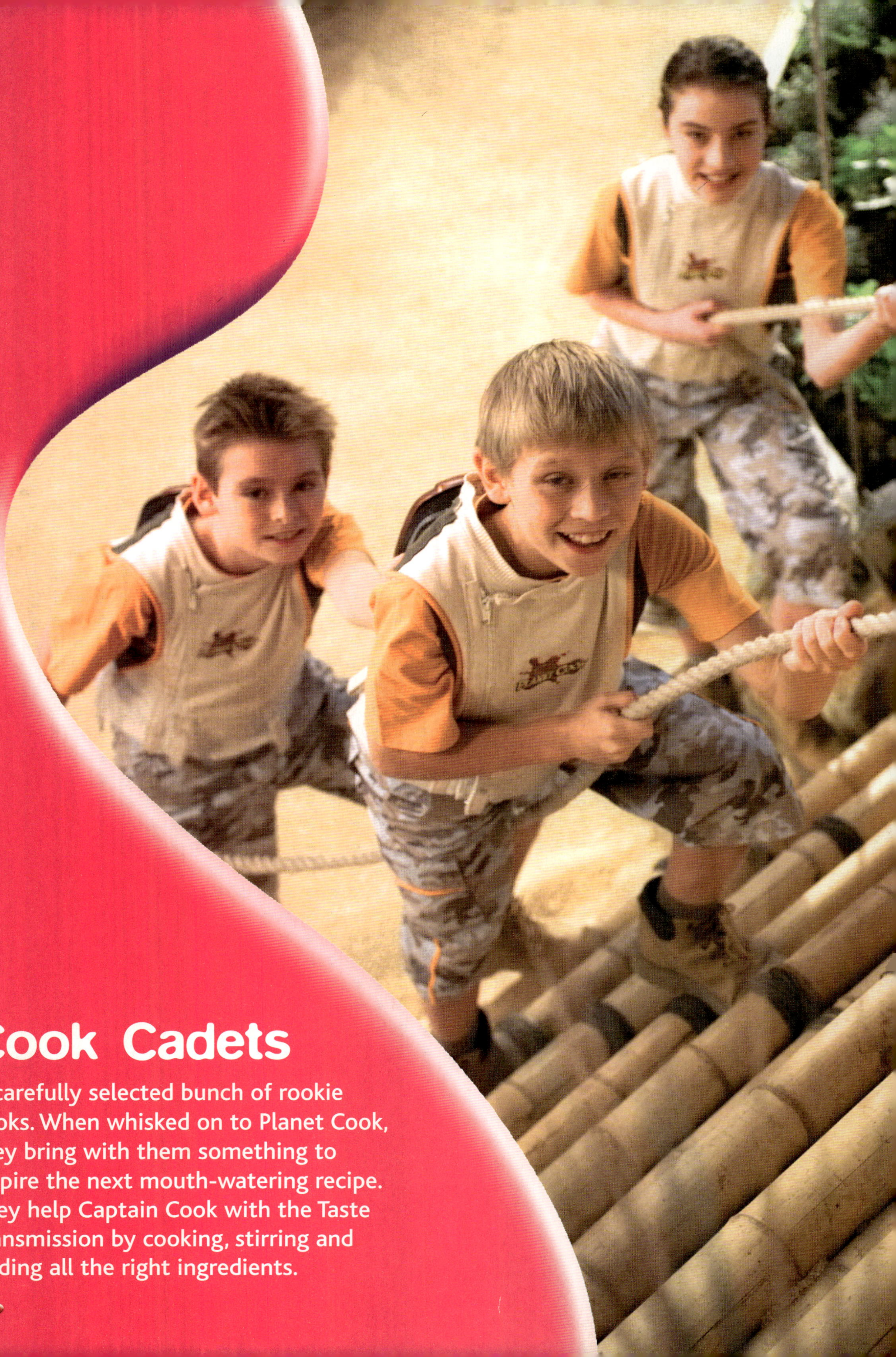

Cook Cadets

A carefully selected bunch of rookie cooks. When whisked on to Planet Cook, they bring with them something to inspire the next mouth-watering recipe. They help Captain Cook with the Taste Transmission by cooking, stirring and finding all the right ingredients.

Roxy

She's the high-tech computer system who shows Captain Cook, the Cook Cadets and Bouma all the 'Info-Bites' – video clips of the natural world - that gives them the inspiration to create a tasty dish for the Taste Transmission. Roxy then transmits the Taste Transmissions all across the world.

DESTINATION

ITALY

What do you think Italy looks like? That's right, it is shaped exactly like a boot, even with a heel and toe! It juts out far into the Mediterranean sea.

In Rome is the Vatican City. This is the home of the Pope and the headquarters of the Catholic Church. It is actually a walled city with its own flag, stamps, national anthem, newspaper and currency!

Apart from penne, spaghetti and ravioli, did you know that there are over 200 different shapes of pasta!

The Colosseum of Rome stands 50 metres high and measures 185 metres long. It was large enough to hold 50,000 spectators when it was inaugurated in 80 AD. Today, it is one of the most dramatic, historic and recognised monuments on earth.

Info-Bite

STROMBOLI

Info-Bite

- Stromboli is one of the Aeolian (ay-e-o-lee-an) Islands of Italy.
- Stromboli is one of the most active volcanoes on Earth.
- A volcano is a big opening in the Earths crust. It's basically a big mountain but with a hole in the top.
- Volcanoes are like giant safety valves that release the pressure that builds up inside the Earth.
- An ACTIVE volcano is one that erupts regularly.
- A DORMANT volcano has not erupted for many years but there is still activity deep inside.
- MAGMA is the liquid rock inside a volcano.
- LAVA is liquid rock that flows out of the volcano.
- The world's largest, ACTIVE volcano is Mauna Loa in Hawaii.
- A Person who studies volcanoes is called a Volcanologist.
- There are more than 1500 active volcanoes on the Earth of which 80 or more are under the oceans.

TASTE TRANSMISSION
VOLCANO SURPRISE

A sprinkle of Inspiration and a Spoonful of Imagination! Let's Cook It!

Volcano Surprise

Baked mash potato and cod volcano with baked bean Lava

1kg (2 lb 4oz) old potatoes
300g (10 oz) cod fillet, boneless and skinless
2 eggs
flour for dusting
dry breadcrumbs
50g (2 oz) Red Leicester cheese – coarsely grated
salt and freshly ground black pepper
1 x 425g (15 oz) baked beans

Preheat oven to 190°C/375°F Gas Mark 5

1

Gather your ingredients together and ask a grown-up to help you. Preheat the oven to 190°C (375°F, Gas Mark 5). Cut the peeled potatoes into even-sized pieces. Rinse them and put them in a saucepan. Cover them with water and bring to the boil. Then put the lid on the pan and simmer for 15 minutes. Drain them and keep them warm.

2

Rinse the fish and pat it dry. Cut the fish into rock-sized nuggets and put them on a plate.

3

Beat one egg in a small bowl. Roll the fish nuggets in the flour. Then dip them in the egg. Finally, roll them in the breadcrumbs to make them look like volcanic rocks.

4

Put the nuggets on a lightly greased baking sheet and grill them until they are golden.

5

Mash the potatoes with the coarsely grated cheese, then add a little pepper. Beat one egg in a bowl and stir almost all of it into the mash mixture. Save a tablespoon of egg for later.

6

Now you can start to build your volcano! Grease a baking sheet and make a base with the mash mixture. Then build up the sides to make a deep hole in the centre.

7

Put the fish nuggets inside the volcano and then finish with the remaining mashed potato. Brush the saved egg over the volcano sides. Put the volcano in the oven for about 20 minutes, until its starts to turn golden brown. Put the baked beans in a saucepan on a low heat.

8

Take the volcano out of the oven and let it stand for a few minutes – your volcano is nearly ready to erupt. Carefully using a large spatula and some help from an adult, place the volcano onto a big serving plate.

9

Quickly pour the baked beans into the centre of the volcano, letting them flow down the sides just like lava.

10

Grab forks and dig in to stop the eruption!

Info-Bite password

LAVA

HOT ROCKS! – Make your own Volcano!

For the volcano:
- a strong piece of board (i.e. hardboard or thick cardboard)
- lots of old newspaper
- aluminium foil
- a test tube or similar thin plastic/glass tube
- paint - brown, green and grey
- sticky tape or glue
- (optional: spray glue, sand and clear varnish)

For the lava:
- a small pot of bicarbonate of soda
- a bottle of vinegar (malt works best)
- red food colouring

1

Securely tape the test-tube to the centre of the piece of card so that the open end is at the top, and the tube stands up vertically on the card, which will act as a base.

2

Build up a cone shape around the test-tube using different sized balls of rolled up newspaper, making sure the top is level with the centre of the tube. Tape or glue the newspaper in place to stop it from coming apart.

3

Once you have created a good cone shape (don't make it too symmetrical), cover the whole structure with aluminium foil. (It's good idea to scrunch the foil up a bit, to give the surface of your volcano some texture.) Secure the foil in place with some sticky tape or glue.

4

Make a hole in the foil where the opening of the test-tube is.

5

You can now make your model look like a real volcano by painting it. Once the paint is dry, the surface can be given an even more realistic texture by spraying it with glue and sprinkling some sand on to it.

6

If you want your volcano to last numerous eruptions over an extended time, you may want to strengthen the surface by giving it a couple of coats of clear varnish.

7

To make you volcano erupt, place a small amount of bicarbonate of soda (half teaspoon) in the bottom of the test-tube. Add a couple of drops of food colouring to some vinegar (~2-4 teaspoons), pour into the test-tube, and watch the thick, bubbly lava flow down your volcano!

DESTINATION

AUSTRALIA

The vast desert area in the middle of Australia is known as The Outback. It is one of the hottest, driest places in the world. Australia is the smallest of the world's seven continents. Australia's Christmas holiday comes in the middle of summer!

Surfing is a favourite sport of Australians. Even surfing carnivals are held regularly in many places.

Ayers Rock (Uluru) is one of the most famous sights in Australia. It's a massive block of sandstone and is 335m (1,142ft) high. The rock is famous for seeming to change colour at sunset when the sun hits it.

Australia has nine sheep for every one person!

Info-Bite

KANGAROO

Info-Bite

- There are more than 50 different kinds of Kangaroos. The smaller ones are usually called Wallabies. The largest is the Red Kangaroo.
- A group of Kangaroos is called a MOB
- Baby Kangaroos are called Joey's. Female Kangaroos are called Doe's or Flyer's and male Kangaroos are called BUCKS.
- Western Grey Kangaroos are known as 'Stinkers' because they have a strong smell, a bit like curry!
- Kangaroos can't walk backwards!
- Kangaroos can reach speeds of over 65kph
- Kangaroos are MARSUPIALS – instead of growing inside their mother's tummy, the babies grow in pouches of skin outside the tummy.
- Kangaroo's are macropods which means "big foot".
- It stands taller than a man and can weigh 85 kg's. It is the largest marsupial in the world.

TASTE TRANSMISSION
KANGAROO POUCHES

A sprinkle of Inspiration and a Spoonful of Imagination!
Let's Cook It!

Kangaroo Pouches

Pitta bread Kangaroo pouches with a honey chicken and pepper filling

---

2 tablespoons honey
300g (12oz) chicken breasts, skinned
1 tablespoon vegetable oil
1 clove garlic, peeled and crushed
1 red pepper, deseeded and thinly sliced
1 tablespoon soy sauce
2 tablespoons tomato ketchup
4 large pitta breads
1 small lettuce, washed and shredded

Cucumber Dip

50g (2oz) cucumber
2 tablespoons mayonnaise
2 tablespoons Greek yogurt
2 tablespoons sweetcorn
salt and freshly ground black pepper

1

Gather your ingredients together and ask a grown-up to help you. Wash the chicken breasts. Then pat them dry and cut them into thin strips. Put them into a bowl. Carefully wash your hands, the chopping board and the knife. This stops bacteria from the raw chicken spreading to other raw ingredients.

2

Add the honey to the chicken and stir it in well.

3

Heat the oil in a wok. Add the chicken strips and fry for 1 minute. Then add the garlic, pepper, ketchup and soy sauce.

4

Cook for 4 to 5 minutes on a medium heat. Check to make sure that the chicken is cooked (there should be no pink colour in the meat). Then take it off the heat and keep it warm.

5
Peel the cucumber and cut it into small cubes.

6
Mix the mayonnaise with the yogurt. Then add the cucumber and sweetcorn, and put the mixture into a dipping bowl.

7

Grill the pitta bread until slightly golden, then cut one pointy end off each pitta. Carefully slide your fingers into the large pieces to open them up into kangaroo pouches.

8

Carefully fill each kangaroo pouch with the chicken and pepper mixture, making sure there is some room left to add your cucumber dip.

9

Arrange each filled kangaroo pouch onto a bed of lettuce on a large serving plate. Don't forget a bowl of cucumber dip!

10

Well done! You've made four little Joeys!

Info-Bite password

JOEY

AUSTRALIAN ANAGRAMS

Can you work out the following anagrams? They all have something to do with Australia. Answers on page 62.

A rook sang

Kang

Saint Laura

Laura's Imp

York races

Risk nets

Hot tub cake

Fin rugs

Rested

WORDSEARCH

Can you find the following words hidden inside the grid. They are hidden forwards, backwards and diagonally. Answers on page 62.

Australia	Kangaroo	Doe	Mob	Outback
Marsupial	Flyer	Buck	Uluru	Stinker

F	O	D	D	E	C	B	L	A	V
L	R	H	O	B	L	U	I	M	O
A	M	O	N	E	F	L	Y	E	R
I	O	S	O	D	A	U	P	L	E
P	B	U	X	R	C	R	O	S	K
U	I	K	T	H	A	U	I	R	N
S	E	S	Q	B	Y	G	A	P	I
R	U	R	L	U	A	I	N	G	T
A	A	S	V	C	E	C	R	A	S
M	B	O	F	K	I	N	K	E	K

TASTE TRANSMISSION GAME

It's a race to get all your ingredients together before the Timer runs out! Each player must start on the taste bud of their choice – Sweet, Sour, Bitter or Salt and then taking it in turns must throw the dice and move around the board trying to land on objects from their menu listed opposite. If you move past an item, don't worry its a big circle and you can go round and round until all your items have been picked up. You will need some counters, a dice and some pieces of paper to check your items off. The winner is the taste bud who collects all their items first.

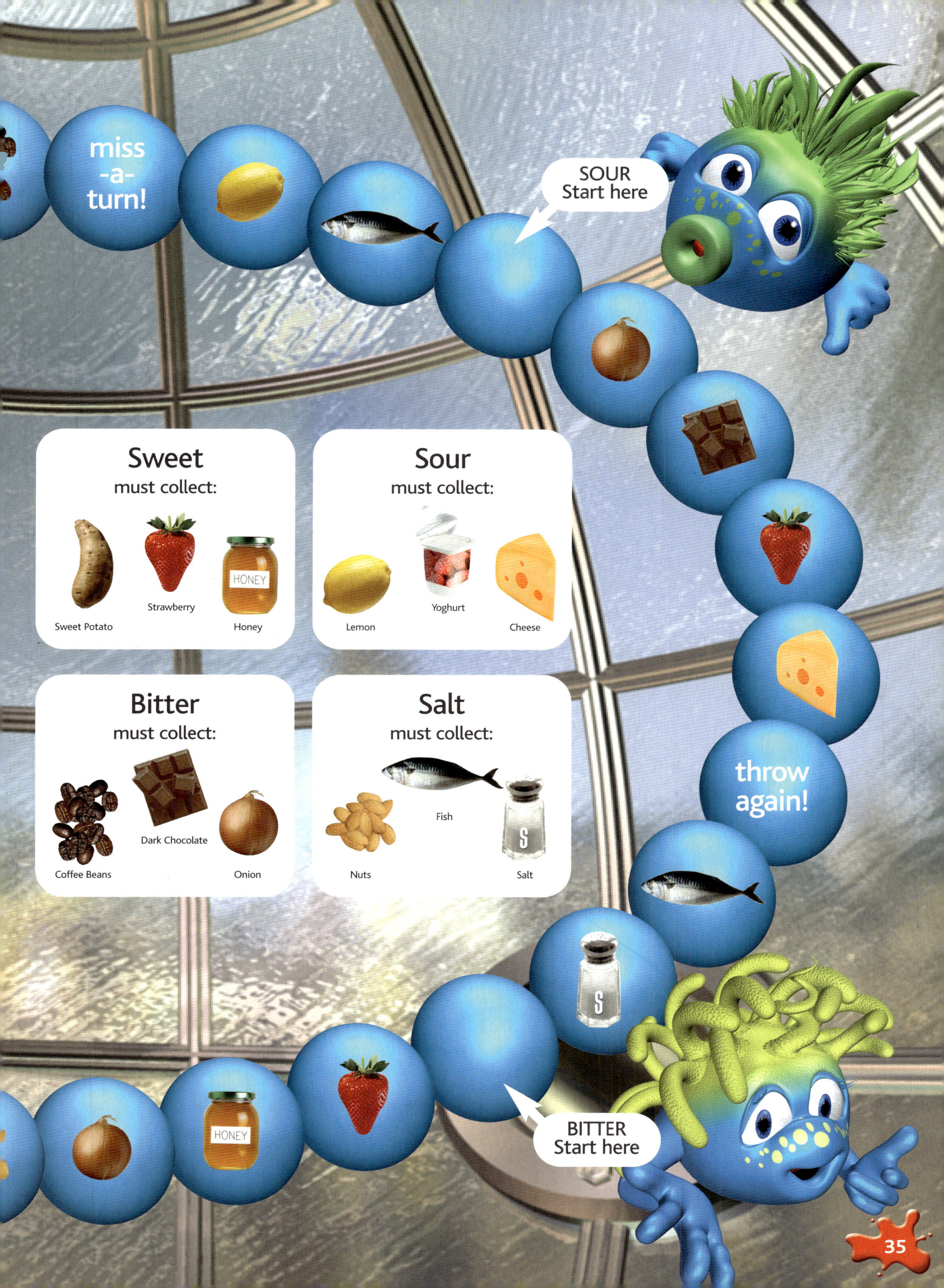
miss -a- turn!
SOUR Start here
Sweet
must collect:
Sweet Potato
Strawberry
HONEY
Honey
Sour
must collect:
Lemon
Yoghurt
Cheese
Bitter
must collect:
Coffee Beans
Dark Chocolate
Onion
Salt
must collect:
Nuts
Fish
Salt
throw again!
HONEY
BITTER Start here

DESTINATION

INDONESIA

Although over 13,000 islands make up the Republic of Indonesia, people only live on about 6,000 of them. Most people live in the countryside and work on farms. Indonesia consists of 300 different ethnic groups.

Elephants in Thailand work very hard and are trained to work for a living. They can live for 30 years and can drag very heavy loads. The elephant is the largest land mammal with 3 species: African savanna, African forest and Asian.

In Bali you could get your change for money back in sweets because the Indonesian Rupiah is worth so little.

Earthquakes and volcanic eruptions can sometimes cause a TSUNAMI. This is a giant wave, which can travel as fast as 800kph!

Info-Bite

OCTOPUS

Info-Bite

- Octopus can change colour anytime they want to hide from their enemies. When they're scared they turn white and when they're angry they turn red!
- They don't like to fight. They use their ink like liquid to trick their enemies. The inky blob looks like the Octopus and when the enemy is attacking that, they swim away
- An Octopus has eight arms called TENTACLES. Each tentacle has 240 suction cups on it.
- If an Octopus gets injured by another animal and loses an arm, another one will grow right back in it's place. Starfish can do this to, it's called REGENERATION.
- One blue-ringed octopus, smaller than your hand, has enough poison to kill many humans.
- Most octopuses are poor swimmers. They usually get around using their arms to crawl along the ocean floor.
- They can squeeze through tiny holes as if they were moving from room to room through keyholes.

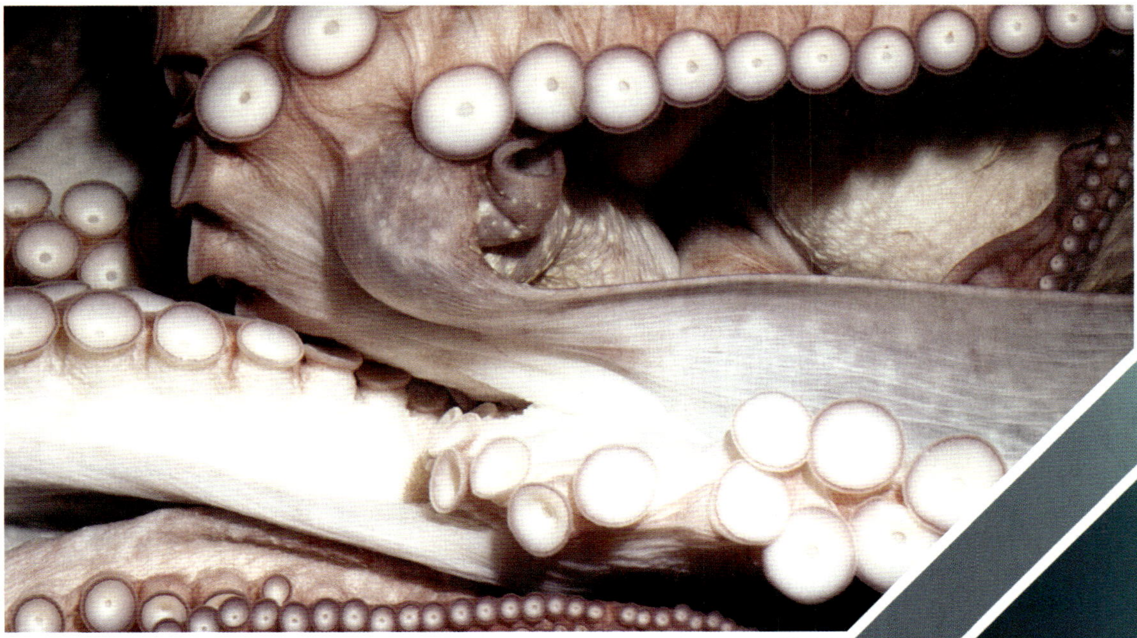

TASTE TRANSMISSION
FRUIT OCTOPUS

A sprinkle of Inspiration and a Spoonful of Imagination! Let's Cook It!

Fruit Octopus with Ice Lolly Suckers

Melon Octopus with home made ice lolly tentacles, serves 8

1 large melon
1 small pineapple
1 small mango
2 passion fruits
100g (4oz) fresh strawberries
2 kiwis

Other ingredients for the octopus tentacle ice lollies:
Juice from 2 oranges
Juice ½ lime.

1

Gather all your ingredients together! Ask a grown-up to help you whenever you need to use a knife. Slice off one end of the melon, so you can stand it up on a large plate. Now you need to make the zig-zag lid. Push the knife in about one quarter of the way down the melon.

2

Then zig-zag through the skin, all the way around the melon, until the top comes off. Well done! You've made the lid!

3

Use a spoon to take out the seeds. Then use a melon baller to cut out half the flesh of the melon. You will use these little balls later!

4

Use a spoon to scoop out the rest of the flesh of the melon. Don't forget to scoop out the inside of the lid! Put it into a blender with 4 strawberries.

5

Ask a grown-up to help you take the skin off the pineapple. Then remove the core and cut the flesh into cubes.

6

Add half the pineapple cubes to the blender. Blend the ingredients until they are smooth.

7

Sieve the blended fruit to get rid of any bits. Then mix the blended fruit with the orange and lime juice. Pour the blended mixture into 8 lolly moulds. Add a lolly stick to each mould. Then put them in the freezer!

8

Cut the rest of the fruit into small pieces (except for 2 strawberries). Mix it together with the melon balls and pineapple cubes you made earlier. Then put the fruit into the hollow melon and put the lid on.

9

Make 8 slits around the base of the melon. When the lollies are frozen, push the wooden sticks into the slits. These are the tentacles! Finally, add the strawberry eyes and serve!

10

Better suck on those lollies before the tentacles suck on you!

Info-Bite password

OCTOPUS

POM POM OCTOPUS

You will need:

- Cardboard
- Compass or two different sized circular items you can trace around.
- Wool – cut into 2 metre lengths
- Scissors

Create two doughnut shaped pieces of cardboard. Using your compass or larger of your two circular items, trace out two circles on your cardboard. About 5cm (2 inches) diameter.

Next put a smaller circle, say 2cm in the middle of your larger circles.

Now cut out the two larger circles, and then carefully cut out the inner circles. You will now have two rings, 5cm outside diameter with a 2cm diameter hole.

Place the rings together.

Hold one end of the wool on the outside of the ring and feed the other end through the hole, round the back and through the front again. Repeat this, working your way around until all the cardboard is covered. When you start with a new piece of wool make sure the ends are on the outside, not in the middle. If it makes it easier, try using a large darning needle to feed the wool through.

Once your rings are fairly full of wool, cut the wool around the edges (the scissor blade should pass between the two pieces of cardboard), this can be tricky so get an adult to help you. You won't be able to cut it all in one go so just do a few layers at a time.

Pass a length of wool between the two pieces of cardboard, around all the strands of wool, and tie it firmly together. Now you can cut and remove the cardboard rings. Trim any lengths of wool which are uneven to give your pom- poms a tidy look. Another idea is a pom-pom 'puppet'. Cut out from felt (or other thick material) pieces for feet, eyes, nose and mouth which can be glued on to make a little 'puppet'. Personalise your Octopus!

DESTINATION

GREENLAND

This is the largest island in the world. People were misled to believe that it had greenery and was a good place to grow crops to make a good living, but in fact, Greenland is a land of snow and ice. It's cold all the time so only the hardest trees can survive.

An estimated two million seals live in the waters here. Walruses are primarily seen in north and east Greenland.

There are icebergs nearly all over Greenland. Icebergs can sometimes be 100 metres above sea level in the Disko Bay. Remember that 90 percent of an iceberg is below the seas surface so think how huge they are!

In late summer and autumn whales can be seen swimming close to the coast. There are various species of whale in the sea including the two largest: the fin whale and the blue whale.

Info-Bite

POLAR BEAR

Info-Bytes

- Polar bears are well-adapted to severe cold. Winter temperatures in the far north often plunge to -40° F or -50° F and can stay that way for days or even weeks.
- Polar bears have two layers of fur for further protection from the cold and their compact ears and small tail also help prevent heat loss.
- Polar bears have more problems with overheating than they do with cold. Even in very cold weather, they quickly overheat when they try to run.
- Each paw measures up to 12 inches across (31 centimetres).
- When the ice is very thin, polar bears crawl on their bellies to keep from breaking through. By crawling, the bears spread out their weight even more.
- The polar bear's large paws are designed for use in the water as well as on the ice. The forepaws serve as large paddles when the bears are swimming, while the hind paws serve as rudders.

TASTE TRANSMISSION
POLAR BEAR PLAICE

A sprinkle of Inspiration and a Spoonful of Imagination! Let's Cook It!

Polar Bear Plaice

A fillet of plaice or sole in a white cheese sauce, with arctic mash potato and salmon carrots.

Arctic Mash
1lb old potatoes, peeled and halved
4 tablespoons warm skimmed milk
2 teaspoons olive oil
pinch of grated nutmeg

Polar bears:
4 fillets plaice, skinned
50mls milk to poach

Cheese sauce:
25g (1oz) butter
25g (1oz) plain flour
280ml (10floz) skimmed milk
50g (2oz) cheddar cheese
salt and white pepper

Garnish
225g (8 oz) carrots, peeled
225g baby spinach
1 tsp olive oil

1

Gather all your ingredients together and ask a grown-up to help you. Preheat the oven to 200°C (400°F, Gas Mark 6). Put the potatoes in a large pan of cold water. Bring the water slowly to the boil. When it is boiling, turn down the heat and put the lid on the pan. Simmer for 25 minutes.

2

Melt the butter in a pan, then add the flour and mix together. Cook over a low heat for 2 minutes. Now add the milk, a little bit at a time. Keep stirring with a wooden spoon. When all the milk has been added, heat until the mixture is bubbling. Take the pan off the heat and stir in the cheese. Add a pinch of salt and white pepper. Then cover the sauce and keep it warm.

3

Roll up the fish into cylinders, with the skinned side inside. Put them into a shallow dish. Then add enough milk to come halfway up the sides of the dish. Now cover the dish with foil and bake for 10 to 15 minutes.

4

Drain the potatoes. Then put them back in the pan over a very low heat. Shake the pan until the potatoes start to break up. Now take them off the heat. Add the olive oil, warm milk and nutmeg. Then beat the potatoes until they are fluffy. Keep them warm.

5

Peel the carrots and cut into 4cm-long pieces. Then cut each piece into quarters lengthways. Add the carrots to a pan of boiling water. Cook them for 2 minutes until they are tender. Drain them and keep them warm.

6

Heat the olive oil in a wok and add the spinach. Press it down with a wooden spoon, then cover with a lid and cook for 1 minute, stirring occasionally. Now drain off as much liquid as you can. Chop the spinach and mix it into the mashed potato.

7

Take the fish out of the oven. Strain the milk into the cheese sauce and drain the fish on kitchen paper. Then warm the sauce over a low heat. Stir the mixture until it is smooth.

8

Pile some of the mashed potato and spinach mix high onto the middle of the plates to look like a like a big lump of ice.

9

Put the 'polar bear' fish onto the plate, leaning on the 'ice'. Pour the cheese sauce over them. Then put the 'salmon' carrots around the polar bear.

10

Well done! You have finished your arctic scene!

Info-Bite password

COLD

LIP SMACKING TONGUE FACTS!

Girls have more taste buds than boys

We have nearly 10,000 taste buds inside our mouths, even on the top of mouths (this is called the roof)

Insects have the most developed taste buds. They have taste organs on their feet and antennae

Without it, you wouldn't be able to eat or speak

Not only is it the strongest muscle in your body, but it is the only muscle that is connected at only one end

Like fingerprints, everyone's tongue print is different

The colour of your tongue can be a good indicator of your health, if it is pale pink, it could mean something has broken down. If you get a yellowish coating over your tongue, it can mean you have a fever, or some kind of digestive complication

A chameleon's tongue is twice the length of its body

A blue whales tongue can weigh more than a small truck and is the length of an elephant

A giraffe has a purple tongue and can clean its own ears with its 40cm-long tongue

Your tongue consists of four different types of taste buds, one of which closely resembles the shape of a mushroom

The world's longest tongue belongs to a woman, it is 9.3 cm long from the tip of her lips when extended

Different areas of your tongue tastes the difference between, sweet, sour, salt and bitter

GREENLAND CROSSWORD

Across:

2) Plant life that grows on frozen ground.

3) A type of plankton eaten by fish.

6) Only the ______ area of Greenland ever turns green.

8) Type of bear whose fur looks white.

9) The coldest area in the world.

Down:

1) Country that used to claim ownership of Greenland.

4) Greenland is the largest ______ in the world.

5) A group of fish is called a ______.

7) The frozen land of the arctic.

8) Bear's feet.

BOUMA'S FUNNY BONES!

What's the worst thing about being an Octopus?

Having to wash your hands!

What can you make with a lump of cheese?

A mouse very happy!

Knock, Knock? Who's there? Lettuce. Lettuce who?

Lettuce in and we'll tell you!

Why do fish stay away from the computer?

So they don't get caught in the Internet!

How does the man in the moon eat his food?

In satellite dishes!

What do cats call mice on skateboards?

Meals on Wheels!

What does an Octopus wear in winter?

A coat of arms!

Answers:

P32. Australian Anagrams

A rook sang – Kangaroos
Saint Laura – Australian
Laura's Imp – Marsupial
York races – Ayers Rock
Risk nets – Stinkers
Hot tub cake – The Outback
Fin rugs – Surfing
Rested – Desert

P33. Wordsearch

F	O	D	D	E	C	B	L	A	V
L	R	H	O	B	L	U	I	M	O
A	M	O	N	E	F	L	Y	E	R
I	O	S	O	D	A	U	P	L	E
P	B	U	X	R	C	R	O	S	K
U	I	K	T	H	A	U	I	R	N
S	E	S	Q	B	Y	G	A	P	I
R	U	R	L	U	A	I	N	G	T
A	A	S	V	C	E	C	R	A	S
M	B	O	F	K	I	N	K	E	K

P59. Greenland Crossword

Across:
2) LICHEN
3) KRILL
6) COASTAL
8) POLAR
9) ARCTIC

Down:
1) DENMARK
4) ISLAND
5) SCHOOL
7) TUNDRA
8) PAWS